FRANKLIN PARK PUBLIC LIBRARY

3 1316 00421 9336

W9-ATB-378

FRANKLIN PARK PUBLIC LIBRARY
FRANKLIN PARK, ILL.

Each borrower is held responsible for all library
material drawn on his card and for fines accruing on
the same. No material will be issued until such fine
has been paid.

All injuries to library material beyond reasonable
wear and all losses shall be made good to the
satisfaction of the Librarian.

**Replacement costs will be
billed after 42 days overdue.**

American Biographies

MEDGAR EVERS

FRANKLIN PARK LIBRARY
FRANKLIN PARK, IL

Ann Weil

Heinemann
LIBRARY

Chicago, Illinois

www.capstonepub.com
Visit our website to find out more information about Heinemann-Raintree books.

To order:
☎ Phone 800-747-4992
💻 Visit www.capstonepub.com
to browse our catalog and order online.

© 2013 Heinemann Library
an imprint of Capstone Global Library, LLC
Chicago, Illinois

All rights reserved. No part of this publication may be reproduced or transmitted in any form or by any means, electronic or mechanical, including photocopying, recording, taping, or any information storage and retrieval system, without permission in writing from the publisher.

Edited by Abby Colich, Megan Cotugno, and Laura Hensley
Designed by Philippa Jenkins
Original illustrations © Capstone Global Library Limited 2011
Illustrated by Oxford Designers and Illustrators
Picture research by Tracy Cummins
Originated by Capstone Global Library Limited
Printed and bound in China by Leo Paper Group

16 15 14 13 12
10 9 8 7 6 5 4 3 2 1

Library of Congress Cataloging-in-Publication Data
Medgar Evers / Ann Weil.
    p. cm.—(American biographies)
  Includes bibliographical references and index.
  ISBN 978-1-4329-6454-2 (hbk.)—ISBN 978-1-4329-6465-8 (pbk.) 1. Evers, Medgar Wiley, 1925-1963—Juvenile literature. 2. African American civil rights workers—Mississippi—Jackson—Biography—Juvenile literature. 3. Civil rights workers—Mississippi—Jackson—Biography—Juvenile literature. 4. National Association for the Advancement of Colored People—Biography—Juvenile literature. 5. Civil rights movements—Mississippi—History—20th century—Juvenile literature. 6. African Americans—Civil rights—Mississippi—History—20th century—Juvenile literature. 7. Mississippi—Race relations—Juvenile literature. 8. Jackson (Miss.)—Biography--Juvenile literature. I. Title.
  F349.J13W45 2012
  323.092—dc23   2011037578
  [B]

Acknowledgments
The author and publishers are grateful to the following for permission to reproduce copyright material: akg-images: p. 13 (RIA Nowosti); AP Images: pp. 9, 17 (Rogelio V. Solis), 22 (Robert Jordan), 32 (Francis H. Mitchell/Ebony Collection), 37 (Jim Bourdier), 39; Corbis: pp. 10 (© CORBIS), 20 (Joseph Schwartz), 23 (© Bettmann), 26 (© Bettmann), 27 (© Bettmann), 34 (© Bettmann), 40 (© CORBIS); Getty Images: pp. 5 (Michael Ochs Archives), 15 (Ed Clark//Time Life Pictures), 25, 28 (Don Cravens/Time Life Pictures), 31 (PhotoQuest), 35 (FPG), 41 (Chip Somodevilla); Library of Congress Prints and Photographs Division: pp. 8, 12, 14, 16, 19; news.com: p. 33 (JAY CLARKE/MIAMI HERALD); The Granger Collection: p. 6.

Cover photograph of Medgar Evers reproduced with permission from Getty Images (Michael Ochs Archive).

Every effort has been made to contact copyright holders of material reproduced in this book. Any omissions will be rectified in subsequent printings if notice is given to the publisher.

Disclaimer
All the Internet addresses (URLs) given in this book were valid at the time of going to press. However, due to the dynamic nature of the Internet, some addresses may have changed, or sites may have changed or ceased to exist since publication. While the author and publisher regret any inconvenience this may cause readers, no responsibility for any such changes can be accepted by either the author or the publisher.

J-B
EVERS
421-9336

Contents

Some words are shown in bold, **like this**.
These words are explained in the glossary.

A Civil Rights Hero and Martyr

There are many heroes in U.S. history. These men and women risked their lives to make the country a better place for everyone. Medgar Evers was one of these heroes.

Mississippi: black and white

Evers was an African American, or black American, dedicated to the idea of **racial** justice, at a time when blacks in his home state of Mississippi were far from free. Black people had the legal right to vote. But men with guns blocked them from voting. Blacks could not sit at a public lunch counter. They could not swim at a public pool. All blacks were at risk of brutal attacks by white **racists**. In Mississippi a white man could kill a black man without fear of going to jail.

A fight for freedom

Medgar Evers showed extraordinary courage by speaking out against a system of **inequality** that so many took for granted. His work to secure voting rights for black people **inspired** fear and hatred among **white extremists**, who wanted to keep blacks "in their place."

Evers knew that these people had put him on a "death list" in the 1950s. Still, he persisted in his work up until the day he was shot and killed outside his home in Mississippi on June 12, 1963. When Evers was **assassinated**, this made him one of the first **martyrs** of the **civil rights** movement.

Medgar Evers once said,
"You can kill a man, but you
can't kill an idea."

Growing Up in Mississippi

Medgar Evers was born on July 2, 1925, in Decatur, Mississippi. His family roots were in the area. Medgar's father's parents were freed **slaves** and owned land. His grandfather, Mike Evers, owned more than 300 acres (121 hectares) of land. But whites had used legal tricks to steal most of that land.

Medgar Evers lived on a small farm similar to this one.

Family farm

Medgar and his family lived on a much smaller farm. They kept a few farm animals. But the farm could not support them. Medgar's father, James, also worked at a sawmill. Medgar's mother, Jessie, worked as a housekeeper for a white family in town. She also took in laundry at home.

Medgar had an older brother, Charles, and two sisters, Elizabeth and Ruth. His mother had been married before and had three older children as well. But Medgar was always closest to Charles. They were best friends growing up, and their friendship stayed strong for all of Medgar's life. The family was poor, but they always had a place to live and enough to eat. Medgar and Charles picked up scrap metal and empty soda bottles to make a little extra money.

Did you know?

Medgar was named for his great-grandfather, Medgar Wright, who was half American Indian. Medgar Wright had been a slave. He was known for being difficult to "control." This refusal to be mistreated seemed to run in the family. It was also present in Medgar's grandparents and his father, James Evers (see page 10).

COLORED

This photo from the 1930s shows a public drinking fountain for blacks.

Jim Crow laws

During the period when Medgar grew up, life in southern states like Mississippi was very difficult for black people.

Between 1877 and 1910, all southern states—and some northern ones—passed laws known as **Jim Crow laws**. These made black Americans second-class citizens.

Segregation was in place in all public places. Schools, buses, hospitals, restaurants, parks, and even cemeteries were separated by **race**. The areas reserved for black people were older and shabbier (more run-down) than those for white people. Sometimes there were no areas for black people at all. Blacks had to use the back entrances to stores. They had to wait until all white customers had been served before it was their turn. They were not allowed to call white people by their first names.

Segregation

The "American dream" of a better life seemed out of reach for southern blacks during this period. Their hard work did not seem to get them any closer.

Still, white people in the South were totally dependent on blacks in order to maintain their lifestyle. Blacks' labor in the cotton fields made white **plantation** owners wealthy. Black women did the cooking and laundry for many white households. They also took care of the babies. And when a white person died, it was a black man who dug his or her grave.

Did you know?

The name "Jim Crow" came from a stage act by a white entertainer. He did an insulting dance in a crude imitation of blacks.

Mississippi police enforced segregation.

Medgar Evers grew up in a small Mississippi town similar to this one.

"Crazy Jim" Evers

Medgar Evers's father, James, was known as "Crazy Jim." He refused to step off the sidewalk when a white person was walking toward him, as blacks in the South were supposed to do. He was a big, tough man who stood up for himself.

In the South during this period, white storeowners often overcharged black customers. The storeowners unfairly assumed black people were not smart enough to correctly figure out their bill. But when a white storeowner tried this on Jim, he pointed out the mistake.

It was considered shocking for a black person to accuse a white person of lying—even when it was obviously true. So the storeowner accused Evers of calling him a liar and went for his gun. Evers took a bottle and smashed it against the counter, ready to use the sharp edge as a deadly weapon. The storeowner was frightened and backed down.

Learning by example

Medgar and Charles witnessed this whole event. They knew that black people in Mississippi were regularly **lynched** for far less than what their father had done. But for some reason, no one took revenge. The two boys learned early on from their father not to let white people run their lives.

This school for black children was on a plantation in Mississippi. School started late in the year because the children worked in the fields picking cotton.

Elementary school

The elementary school Medgar went to was a one-room shack with a leaky roof. About 100 students from grades one through eight crammed into that one room with two teachers.

There were no school buses in Mississippi for black children. They had to walk to school, no matter how far it was. The high school for black children was 12 miles (19 kilometers) from Medgar's home. Some white school bus drivers would veer to the side and make the black children jump off the road.

Lynching

When Medgar was in elementary school, a family friend was lynched. A white mob dragged him through the streets behind a wagon. Then they killed him. They said he had looked at a white woman and insulted her. Whites often used this excuse for killing a black man.

But as far as the sheriff and police were concerned, lynching was not a crime. They made no arrests. Later, Medgar recalled how the killers had left the dead man's bloody clothes on a fence as a warning to other blacks. He remembered: "Every **Negro** in town was supposed to get the message from those clothes and I can see those clothes now in my mind's eye."

Despite these events, Medgar's mother told him not to hate the white **racists**. She said that hate was a poison. It would hurt him more than it would hurt anyone else.

Violence against black people was common in the South until the 1960s.

From Soldier to Activist

In 1943 Medgar Evers dropped out of high school to join the U.S. Army. He served in England and France during World War II (1939–1945).

The Tuskegee airmen were African American fighter group pilots who flew during World War II.

Another country, another way of life

While he was a soldier, Evers dated a French girl. He spent time with her family. Evers had never socialized with white people before. This new experience showed him that it was possible for whites and blacks to live together as equals. Evers was in love, but he knew he could not return to Mississippi with a white bride, even if she was from another country.

An African American GI dances with a French girl.

A hostile homecoming

Evers returned home a changed man. His experiences overseas had given him hope. He saw that a new way of life was possible for blacks and whites. But he quickly saw that nothing had changed in Mississippi.

When he and his brother, Charles, went to vote, armed men blocked their way to the **polls**. The law said that black people had the right to vote. But that did not matter in Mississippi, where white **racists** were in power.

Evers and his brother left without voting. "All we wanted to be was ordinary citizens," he declared years later. "We fought during the war for America and Mississippi was included. Now after the Germans and the Japanese hadn't killed us, it looked as though the white Mississippians would."

College

Evers finished high school. Then, in 1948, he enrolled at Alcorn College, in Lorman, Mississippi, where he majored in business. Evers was a good student and worked hard at school. He continued to read a lot. He also worked on the college newspaper.

Evers was also athletic and excelled at sports. He was on the football team and ran track. By his junior year, Evers was one of the most popular students on campus. And that was also when he first saw a young freshman named Myrlie.

This photo shows Alcorn College around 1950.

Marriage

Myrlie Beasley grew up in Vicksburg, Mississippi. She had come to Alcorn College to study music. She and Evers started dating. They got married on Christmas Eve in 1951. Myrlie was 18 years old. Evers was 26 and a college senior. He graduated from Alcorn one year later.

Evers lived in this house in Jackson, Mississippi, with his wife Myrlie.

Work

Evers's first job was to sell **life insurance** to blacks who lived in the Mississippi **Delta**. Evers and Myrlie moved to an all-black town called Mound Bayou.

A black doctor named T.R.M. Howard owned the insurance company Evers worked for. Howard helped start a new organization in Mississippi to help black people challenge **Jim Crow laws**. This organization urged blacks to avoid businesses that treated them poorly.

Did you know?

Howard's group had a slogan, which it put on bumper stickers: "Don't buy gas where you can't use the restroom." It took a lot of courage for black people to put these stickers on their cars. Whites might lash out at them and beat them up, or worse, because of that bumper sticker.

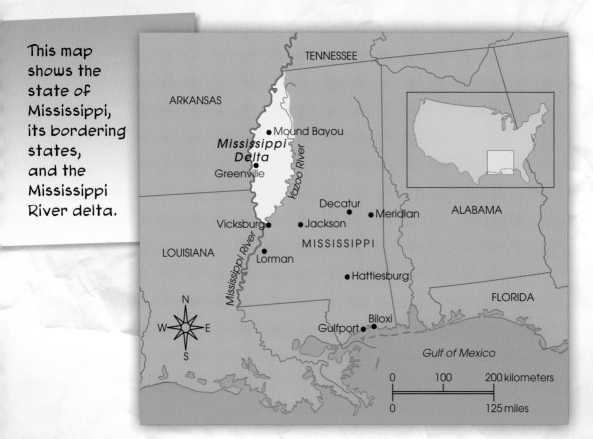

This map shows the state of Mississippi, its bordering states, and the Mississippi River delta.

Sharecropping in the Mississippi Delta

For his job, Evers drove all across the Mississippi Delta (see the map). These travels allowed Evers to see a new side of the black experience in Mississippi.

Many of the people Evers saw were **sharecroppers**. These black farmers did not own their land, as Evers's family had. Rather, they rented land from **plantation** owners. The plantation owners cheated the black sharecroppers out of any profits they might make (see the box).

Plantation owners were often cruel, brutal racists. There were many **lynchings** in the Mississippi Delta region. Sharecroppers lived in fear of their white landlords, just as their **slave ancestors** had. They also lived in some of the worst conditions of **poverty** Evers had ever seen.

Did you know?

The sharecropping system was one of many ways white plantation owners took advantage of blacks after **slavery** ended. White landowners rented land to black farmers. They loaned the blacks money at the beginning of the growing season to buy seeds and other things they needed. White plantation owners overcharged the sharecroppers, most of whom could not read or write. That way the whites could be sure that the black farmers could never pay back the loans. This debt made it illegal for sharecroppers to leave. They had to stay and work on the large plantations. The white plantation owners got richer, while the black sharecroppers got poorer.

Sharecroppers often lived in conditions no better than those of slaves.

The Fight for Civil Rights

Inspired by his experiences, Evers decided to work to bring the **civil rights** movement to Mississippi.

The NAACP

Evers had joined the **National Association for the Advancement of Colored People** (**NAACP**; see the box) back when he was at Alcorn College. He remained an active member after college. Evers encouraged other blacks in Mississippi to join. This was one way he hoped to improve their lives.

This NAACP parade took place in Brooklyn, New York, in the 1940s.

Evers's work brought new branches of the NAACP to the Mississippi **Delta**. By the end of 1953, the NAACP had 21 branches in Mississippi. The total membership was 1,600 people. At that time, Mississippi was home to about a million black people. It was a small start, but the group's membership would grow.

Evers becomes a father

Myrlie and Medgar's first son, Darrell Kenyatta, was born in 1953. A year later their daughter, Rena Denise, was born. Later, in 1960, another son, James, would be born. Evers's family was growing. His children inspired him to work even harder for civil rights.

Did you know?

The NAACP was started in 1909. A group of white people was horrified by the violence they saw against black Americans. They wanted to help blacks get equal protection under the law. There were about 60 founding members, both white and black. The organization grew over the years. By the 1950s, there were more than half a million members all over the country.

Integrating schools took years to achieve. Today, black and white students attend "Ole Miss" together.

"Separate but equal" is not equal

Before 1954, states could have separate schools for black students as long as they were equal to the schools white students attended. But it was obvious to everyone that these schools were far from equal. Evers took photographs that showed the horrible conditions of the black schools in the Mississippi Delta.

This situation changed when the U.S. Supreme Court heard a case known as *Brown v. Board of Education*. The Supreme Court declared that school **segregation** was no longer legal. But Mississippi was still controlled by white **racists**. They did not let blacks vote, even though that was law. They were not going to go along with this court decision either.

Shut out of law school

Evers had already challenged the unfair practice of keeping blacks away from the **polls**. Now he was going to work to **integrate** schools in Mississippi. He thought the best way to do this was to become a lawyer.

Evers applied for admission to the University of Mississippi ("Ole Miss") Law School. Myrlie wondered how they could support their family if Medgar was in law school. Evers told his wife, "We have to make sacrifices to make progress." In the end, though, Evers was denied admission.

Thurgood Marshall

(1908–1993)

Thurgood Marshall was the lead lawyer in the *Brown v. Board of Education* case. In 1967 President Lyndon Johnson appointed him to become the first black justice on the Supreme Court (the highest court in the U.S.). Marshall retired from the Court in 1991.

Last farewell to a father

Evers and his father did not always agree on everything. But Jim Evers was still his son's hero for the way he lived his life. When Evers got a call that his father was dying, he rushed to the hospital.

Black patients did not get rooms at the hospital like white patients did. They were put down in the basement instead. Evers found his father in the basement and sat at his bedside. When Evers went outside for air, he witnessed an attempted **lynching**. A black man had come to the hospital with a bullet wound in his leg. An armed and angry white mob was outside yelling for the man.

Recalling that night

Later, Evers told about that night in 1954: "The mob was outside the hospital, armed with pistols and rifles, yelling for the **Negro**.... It seemed that this would never change. It was that way for my Daddy, it was that way for me, and it looked as though it would be that way for my children."

Evers returned to his father's deathbed and sat with him until the end. Evers's experience at the hospital was yet more proof that a black American could not live or die in peace in Mississippi. And this was something Evers vowed to change. In the next phase of his career, Evers would find new ways to achieve equal rights for all.

Medgar was already a father himself when his own father died. In this 1953 photo, Medgar is holding his first son, Darrell Kenyatta.

"M Is for Mississippi and Murder"

Evers had been working with the **NAACP** for years. In 1954 the organization offered him a full-time job. Evers and his family moved to Jackson, Mississippi, to open a new NAACP office there. Myrlie was his secretary.

About 50,000 people viewed the body of Emmett Till at his funeral in Chicago. His mother insisted on an open casket even though his face had been destroyed. She wanted the world to see what her son's murderers had done.

Emmett Till

(1941–1955)

Fourteen-year-old Emmett
Till lived in Chicago,
Illinois. Many blacks
from Mississippi had
moved to Chicago, where
there were jobs and no
Jim Crow laws. In 1955
Till came with a cousin
to the **Delta** town of
Money, Mississippi, to
visit relatives. One evening Till was out with his
cousin and some other young blacks. Till whistled at a white woman.
He did not mean any harm. Young men whistled at pretty women in
Chicago all the time. But this act was very serious in Mississippi.

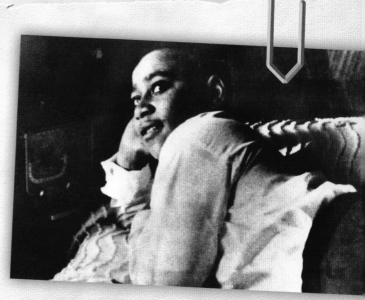

Later, the woman's husband and a friend went to the house where
Till was staying. They kidnapped him at gunpoint. The next time
Till's family saw him, he was dead. The head of the NAACP called the
murder a **lynching**. This was the violent world to which Evers was
trying to bring change.

Before this NAACP office opened, black people in Mississippi
had no one to turn to when they were the victims of **racial**
violence. The police did not protect blacks from violence, and
they did not investigate crimes against blacks.

In his new role, Evers investigated crimes against black
people himself. Sometimes Evers disguised himself as a
sharecropper. Sometimes he borrowed someone else's car,
because the police would recognize his license plate.

African Americans walked to work every day for more than a year during the 1956 bus boycott in Montgomery, Alabama.

Protests and boycotts

In addition to investigating racial violence, Evers organized **boycotts**. He also encouraged nonviolent **sit-ins**. Blacks would sit down at a white-only lunch counter, or go to a white library and sit down there. Doing this took courage. They were often **assaulted** or arrested. Evers and other **civil rights activists** believed that such actions would help their cause.

Sit-in on the bus

One day in 1958, Evers was taking a bus back home to Jackson, Mississippi, after working in another town. Evers had encouraged other blacks to demand their rights, so he did the same. Evers sat in the front of the bus. The bus driver ordered him to move to the back, which was where blacks were supposed to sit. Evers refused.

The bus driver called the police. They asked to see Evers's identification. He showed it to them. Then the police took him to the police station. They asked if he was trying to make trouble. Evers told them no, he was just trying to get home to his wife and children. They let him go.

Back on the bus

Evers got back on the bus. Again he sat in the front seat. Again the bus driver ordered him to move back. Again Evers refused. Finally, the bus drove on. A few blocks later, a white man got on the bus. He punched Evers in the face. Evers did not hit back. He knew that any violent reaction against whites would be blown out of proportion and fuel more racial violence.

The power of the vote

During this period the southern whites in power did everything they could to keep blacks "in their place." Evers knew that this could only change if more blacks in Mississippi voted. But whites did not want blacks to vote. They targeted blacks who registered to vote with increasing violence.

Activist or troublemaker?

Evers always said he was working to make Mississippi a better place for *all* people, not just blacks. But many middle-class blacks in Mississippi did not appreciate what he was trying to do. They were afraid that his actions would stir up trouble. Some blacks even spied on Evers. They kept track of what he did and where he went. Then they reported this to the police.

Did you know?

The 14th Amendment to the Constitution granted full citizenship rights to ex-**slaves**. That included the right to vote. But some states required voters to take a test and pay something called a **poll** tax. These tactics were used to keep black people from voting.

These citizens were registering to vote in Greensboro, Alabama, in 1956. In Mississippi, blacks who registered to vote risked their lives.

George W. Lee

(1904–1955)

On May 7, 1955, in Mississippi, a black man named George Lee was shot in the face while driving his car. The police said it was a traffic accident. But experts found evidence of pellets from a gun in his face and car tires. Lee was one of the names on a "death list" published by **white extremists**. Lee was murdered because he refused to take his name off the list of registered voters.

The Murder of Medgar Evers

Evers worked closely with black church leaders and other **civil rights activists**. After he appeared on television, everyone knew his face. Many people made death threats against Evers and his family. Myrlie answered some of these calls at the office and at home.

Medgar and Myrlie Evers with their daughter Rena and son Darrell visit the Civil War battlefield at Vicksburg in 1958.

Firebomb!

In May 1963, Myrlie was waiting up for her husband, who was working late, as usual. He often worked as much as 20 hours a day. The children were in bed. Myrlie heard the crash of a bottle breaking outside, then a *whoosh* as flames exploded. She was terrified. She thought someone was waiting outside to shoot them. But she had to put the fire out. She ran outside and doused the flames with the garden hose. Luckily, Evers had taught his children to fall to the floor whenever they heard a strange noise outside.

Myrlie's thoughts

Later, Myrlie said, "Medgar knew what he was doing, and he knew what the risks were. He just decided that he had to do what he had to do. But I knew at some point in time that he would be taken from me."

This statue of Medgar Evers was built in Jackson, Mississippi, in 1992.

Murder

On June 11, 1963, President John F. Kennedy gave a speech in support of civil rights. It was on television and the radio. Hours later, Evers lay dying in the driveway of his home in Jackson, Mississippi.

Evers was getting out of his car when he was shot in the back with a high-powered deer rifle. He was holding a bunch of "**Jim Crow** Must Go" T-shirts when he fell. Myrlie and the children had been waiting up for him to come home.

"I opened the door, and there was Medgar at the steps, face down in blood," Myrlie later told an interviewer. "The children ran out and were shouting, 'Daddy, get up!'" Neighbors gathered. Someone took Evers to the hospital, where he died less than an hour later.

Byron De La Beckwith is escorted by an FBI agent into Jackson City Hall after being arrested on suspicion of murdering Medgar Evers.

The murder weapon and a suspect

The Jackson, Mississippi, police did not investigate Evers's murder. But the Federal Bureau of Investigation (FBI) did.

The gun that was used to kill Evers was found very near the scene of the crime. There was a fingerprint on the gun. It belonged to a man named Byron De La Beckwith. There were witnesses, too. They had seen Beckwith in the Evers's neighborhood on the night of the murder. Beckwith was a member of a **white extremist** group called the **Ku Klux Klan**. He was one of the white extremists who supported the "death list" of people who challenged **segregation**.

Members of the Ku Klux Klan (KKK) bullied and killed blacks and whites who disagreed with them. The group still exists today.

From "not guilty"...

Beckwith had a lot of important friends in Jackson. When he was brought to trial in 1964, a police officer swore that he saw Beckwith that night miles away from where the shooting took place. The all-white male jury found Beckwith innocent.

Myrlie was expecting that verdict. She had lived in Mississippi her whole life. She knew the system was unjust. But she wasn't going to let Beckwith get away with murder. There was a second trial. Again, however, Beckwith was found not guilty.

...to "guilty"

A third trial took place in Mississippi in 1994. This time the faces of the jury were a mix of black and white. There were women sitting in the jury box as well as men. This jury found Byron De La Beckwith guilty of the murder of Medgar Evers.

It took more than 30 years, but Evers's killer was finally put behind bars. Justice was late in coming, but it had finally arrived. Beckwith died in prison in 2001, while serving a life sentence for the murder of Evers.

The "gentlemen of the jury" for the second trial of Byron De La Beckwith, shown leaving the courthouse, found him not guilty.

NO CAMERAS OR RECORDING EQUIPMENT ALLOWED IN BUILDING DEPOSIT IN

After Medgar, No More Fear

Medgar Evers was the first well-known person **assassinated** because of his work to promote the **civil rights** of black Americans. His death marked a change in the way people thought about civil rights. Evers was buried in Arlington National Cemetery, in Virginia, next to soldiers and historical figures who had given their lives for their country.

"...no more fear..."

Now the entire country began to look at what was going on in Mississippi and the rest of the South. A magazine writer summed it up this way: "People who lived through those days will tell you that something shifted in their hearts after Medgar Evers died, something that put them beyond fear.... At that point a new motto was born: 'After Medgar, no more fear.'"

Leaving a legacy of nonviolence

After Evers's funeral in Jackson, thousands of mourners marched behind the funeral procession. But their grief was mixed with anger over Evers's murder.

Things began to turn violent. A brave lawyer who had worked with Evers in the past tried to stop the violence before it got out of control. Someone handed him a bullhorn so that he could be heard over the screaming crowd. He reminded them that Evers chose to avoid violent confrontations. It was not the way to win. His words calmed the crowd, and they did not riot. They agreed that violence wasn't the right way to remember their hero.

Medgar Wiley Evers was buried on June 19, 1963, in Arlington National Cemetery. He received full military honors in front of a crowd of more than 3,000 people.

Continuing his legacy

Myrlie sought justice for Medgar's murder. She also took up
her husband's fight to make Mississippi and the United States
a better place for black Americans—and for all Americans.
After her husband's death, Myrlie became more active in
the struggle for civil rights. Eventually she became the
chairperson of the national board of the **NAACP**.

Mayor Charles Evers

Evers's brother, Charles, also fought for the issues that
were important to his brother. He ran for mayor of Fayette,
Mississippi. He used the slogan, "Hands that picked cotton
can now pick the mayor." Thanks to the Voting Rights Act of
1965, blacks had more rights, freedom, and security than they
had during his brother's lifetime.

Charles Evers
was elected
mayor of
Fayette in 1969.
That made
him the first
black mayor in
Mississippi since
the late 1800s.

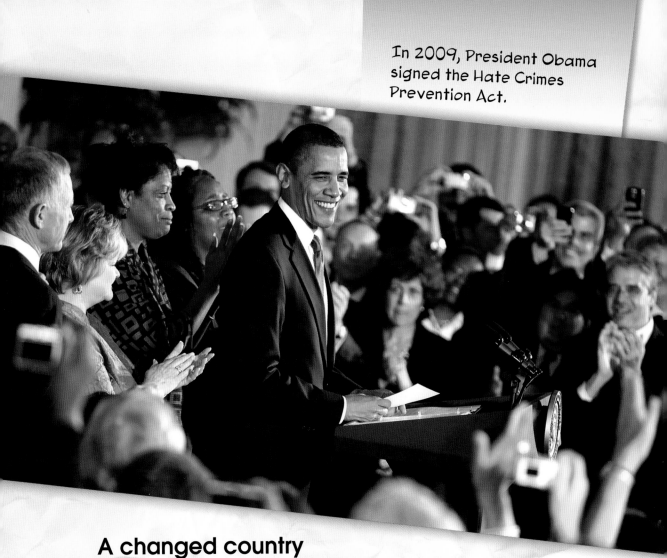

In 2009, President Obama signed the Hate Crimes Prevention Act.

A changed country

While tension and challenges still remain, the United States of today is very different from the one Medgar Evers knew. In 2009 Barack Obama became the first black president of the United States. Myrlie Evers supported Obama's campaign. Thanks to laws such as 2009's Hate Crimes Prevention Act, the sort of violence that led to Evers's murder is no longer tolerated.

Looking back at the changes in society since her husband's death, Myrlie said: "I hope that you will feel a kind of ecstasy in your heart that we have reached this point in American society." Thanks to the sacrifices of people like Medgar Evers, equal rights for all **races** in the United States is no longer just a dream.

Timeline

1925
Medgar Evers is born on July 2 in Decatur, Mississippi.

1930
Evers begins school at Decatur Consolidated School.

1933
Myrlie Beasley is born in Vicksburg, Mississippi.

1941
The Japanese bomb Pearl Harbor (Hawaii). The United States enters World War II (1939-1945).

1943
Evers drops out of high school and joins the U.S. Army at age 17.

1951
Evers marries Myrlie Beasley on Christmas Eve.

1948
Evers enrolls at Alcorn State College to study business.

1947
Evers finishes high school.

1946
Evers tries to vote, but armed white men refuse to let him pass.

1945
Evers returns to Decatur after the war.

1952
Evers graduates from Alcorn College.
Evers takes a job selling life insurance to blacks.
Evers begins recruiting members for the NAACP.

1953
Myrlie and Medgar's first son, Darrell Kenyatta, is born.
Evers begins voter registration drives.

1954
Myrlie and Medgar's daughter, Rena Denise, is born.
The U.S. Supreme Court rules in *Brown v. Board of Education* and declares that state laws for separate black and white schools are unconstitutional.
Evers is denied admission at "Ole Miss" Law School. Evers and his family move to the city of Jackson, Mississippi.
Evers is hired as the first NAACP field secretary for Mississippi.

1955
Fourteen-year-old Emmett Till is murdered in Mississippi.

1960
Myrlie and Medgar's last child, James Van Dyke, is born.

1961
The NAACP's "Operation Mississippi" begins.

1994
Byron De La Beckwith begins his prison term for the murder of Medgar Evers.

1964
Myrlie and the children move to California.
The Civil Rights Act passes, making many forms of segregation and discrimination illegal.

1963
Evers is gunned down in the driveway of his home in Jackson, Mississippi.

Family Tree

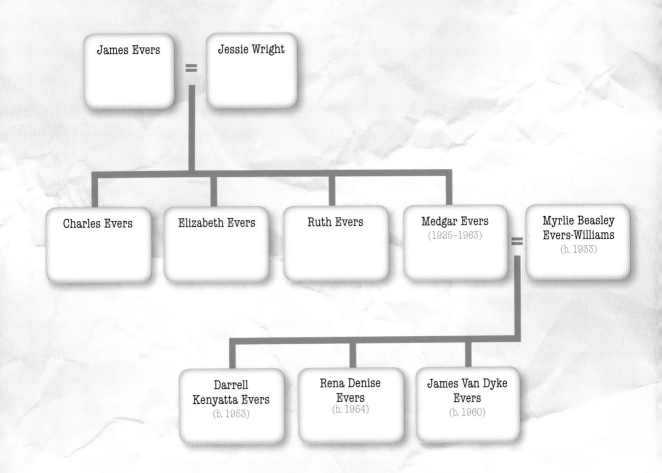

James Evers = Jessie Wright

Charles Evers

Elizabeth Evers

Ruth Evers

Medgar Evers
(1925-1963)

= Myrlie Beasley
Evers-Williams
(b. 1933)

Darrell
Kenyatta Evers
(b. 1953)

Rena Denise
Evers
(b. 1954)

James Van Dyke
Evers
(b. 1960)

Glossary

activist person who speaks or acts to help a group of people or some other cause

ancestor person from whom one is descended; a relative who was born before you

assassinate to kill, often for political reasons

assault attack or physically hurt someone

boycott stop doing something, such as taking a bus, to show dislike or disagreement with a law or action

civil rights equal rights for all Americans

delta area of land near the mouth of a river

inequality condition of being unequal, or treated as less than someone else

inspire to give someone encouragement to do something

integrate allow people of different ethnic or racial groups to be together at public places, schools, work, and social gatherings

Jim Crow laws laws created to keep the races separate and discriminate against black people

Ku Klux Klan secret organization of white racists who hid their identities by wearing hoods and sheets

life insurance policy that protects a person's family by giving them money, or benefits, after the person dies

lynch to kill someone for something he or she supposedly did; lynching is usually performed by a mob, or group, without legal authority

martyr person who dies for something he or she believes in

National Association for the Advancement of Colored People (NAACP) group that works to protect the rights of black Americans

Negro name for black people that was used in the past

plantation large farm where crops are grown

polls place where people vote

poverty situation of being very poor

race group of people who share the same characteristics such as skin color and whose distant relatives come from the same area

racial having to do with race

racist person who believes their own race is better than others

segregation forced separation of races

sharecropper farmer who works for a landowner, and who receives only a small part of the money earned from the crops

sit-in type of nonviolent protest in which people sit in a business or street until they are forced to leave

slave person who has his or her life, liberty, and fortune controlled by another person

slavery relationship in which one person has absolute power over another and controls his or her life, liberty, and fortune

white extremist person who thinks white people are better than nonwhite people

Find Out More

Books

Bowers, Rick. *Spies of Mississippi: The True Story of the Spy Network that Tried to Destroy the Civil Rights Movement.* Washington, D.C.: National Geographic, 2010.

Coleman, Wim, and Pat Perrin. *Racism on Trial: From the Medgar Evers Murder Case to Ghosts of Mississippi* (Famous Court Cases that Became Movies). Berkeley Heights, N.J.: Enslow Publishers, 2009.

Nelson, Marilyn. *A Wreath for Emmett Till.* Boston: Houghton Mifflin, 2009.

Websites

www.NAACP.org
The NAACP
Website has information on the group's history and civil rights work.

http://pbskids.org/aaworld/index.html
African American World for Kids
Visit this website to learn more about important events in African American history.

http://pbskids.org/wayback/civilrights/features_school.html
School Desegregation
Learn about nine brave students who stood up against school segregation during the civil rights movement in 1957.

www.loc.gov/teachers/classroommaterials/themes/civil-rights/students.html
Civil Rights for Students
This Library of Congress website has information and primary source materials about the civil rights time period.

Places to visit

Medgar Evers Home Museum
2332 Margaret Walker Alexander Dr.
Jackson, MS 39213
www.everstribute.org/index.php

Bronze Statue of Medgar Evers
4215 Medgar Evers Blvd.
Jackson, MS 39213
601-982-2867
www.discoverourtown.com/MS/Jackson/Attractions/bronze-statue-of-medgar-evers/176444.html

National Civil Rights Museum
450 Mulberry St.
Memphis, TN 38103
901-521-9699
www.civilrightsmuseum.org/

Brown v. Board of Education Historic Site
1515 SE Monroe St.
Topeka, KS 66612
785-354-4273
www.nps.gov/brvb/index.htm

Index